Love,
VaVa

Va Va Lessons

BOOK III

Va Va Learns About Safety

By

Renee Duane

Illustrated by

Cherie Monteferrante

ISBN: 978-1-970024-32-6

Va Va Lessons

BOOK III

Va Va Learns About Safety

You can call me "Vava."

Most people do because they can't say my name.

My name, Vasishta (Vah see sh ta) is hard to pronounce

Vasishta means "Bringer of Light."

Mommy tells me someday I will understand the meaning of my name.

I live in a big house.

Daddy takes a shower early in the morning.

I can't wait until he steps out.

I scamper in and watch the drops of water run down the wall.

I can spend a long time watching the water drops.

I want to know where the water goes.

Sometimes, I sit in the window and watch the birds.

Do you ever wish you could fly like a bird?

I do.

Recently, I saw a mother bird building her nest right outside my window.

It was really cool how she brought twigs to make the nest.

A few days later she saw me sitting in the window.

I was so excited to see her that my tail moved back and forth quickly and I meowed.

Mother bird flew away.

I've not seen her since.

I don't know why she hasn't returned.

Some days, I like to sit on Mommy's desk and watch her computer screen.

She puts on *You Tube* animal shows for me.

I bat at things that move on the screen with my paw.

I like to look at the pictures from my books on the computer too.

Computers are fun.

Do you like to play outside?

At my house we have a big screened area around the pool in the backyard.

I like to go out there and pretend I'm a hunter.

We have little lizards that run fast.

But, I'm faster. Lizards are easy for kitties to catch.

I have a soft mouth.

I try not to hurt the lizard.

Often after I catch the lizard and play a bit, I get bored.

Then, I usually take a nap in the warm sun.

Once my eyes close, the lizard runs away.

One day a little snake found its way into my play area.

I was having great fun batting at it with my paw.

All of a sudden Mommy rushed towards me screaming,

"Va Va, what are you doing?"

She was upset.

"That snake could be poisonous!"

Gosh, I hadn't thought about that.

Mommy used a broom and chased the snake outside.

When Mommy came back, she said,

"Va Va it would be a good idea to check with me first, before you play with something you've never seen before."

Playing with the snake could have been very dangerous for me!

Being bitten by a poisonous snake would not have been good.

Mommy was right. I should ask her before I play with something unfamiliar.

Another day I was napping on the lanai.

I woke up and saw a big bug.

It was running on the other side of the pool.

I thought, *I need to catch that bug.*

I'm Va Va The Hunter.

I jumped up and ran as fast as I could around the pool.

In my hurry to catch the bug,

I missed the corner of the pool.

And, you guessed it,

I fell in!

I don't know how to swim!

In a panic, I started moving my legs quickly.

I had to get out of the pool.

The water was deep.

I tried jumping out of the pool.

But I couldn't jump on water.

I was getting tired.

I was really scared.

Have you ever been really scared?

I knew I couldn't keep thrashing about,

I didn't have the energy.

Finally, I had no choice but to relax my legs.

What's this?

I felt my front and back legs begin to gently paddle.

I was swimming!

I didn't know I could swim.

I worked my way to the side of the pool.

With the bit of strength I had left, I dragged myself out of the water.

Phew! What a relief to be on solid ground again.

That was very frightening for me when I fell in the pool.

I asked myself, *What did I learn from that experience besides the fact that I can swim?*

I learned it's not good to run around a pool because you just might fall in.

I was really lucky I didn't drown.

CPSIA information can be obtained
at www.ICGtesting.com
Printed in the USA
BVOW05*2104150617
486849BV00005B/6/P

9 781970 024326